Original title:
The Meaning of Life in 5 Minutes or Less

Copyright © 2025 Creative Arts Management OÜ
All rights reserved.

Author: Robert Ashford
ISBN HARDBACK: 978-1-80566-202-0
ISBN PAPERBACK: 978-1-80566-497-0

Life's Lessons by the Minute

Life's a ride, quick and spry,
Chasing dreams as they flutter by.
Laughing hard, then tripping fast,
Sip your coffee, make it last.

Time flies by with a wink and grin,
Tick-tock tales where we begin.
Take a leap, avoid the fall,
Count the wins, ignore the small.

Moonlit nights bring silly thoughts,
Pie in the face, life's funny spots.
Grab your friends for a silly dance,
Embrace the chaos, take a chance.

In each minute, there's laughter stored,
Life's a buffet, go for second course!
So chase delight, let worries cease,
In every heartbeat, find your peace.

Time's Ephemeral Treasures

Life's just a game of peekaboo,
One minute here, next minute adieu.
Joke about it, laugh out loud,
Don't let the mundane make you cowed.

Grab a cookie, melt it slow,
Dance in circles, let chaos flow.
Chasing sunsets, pick a fight,
With gravity, in joyful flight!

Moments blink like fireflies,
Catch the giggles, say your goodbyes.
Life's sweet syrup, sticky fun,
Pour it out, now you're on the run.

So here's a toast, to each misstep,
Moments dance, give life pep.
In hues of laughter, let's invest,
Our fleeting joys, they're simply the best!

Brevity and Brilliance

Short and snappy, life's a fling,
Catch those smiles, let your heart sing.
Tickle the fancies, chase the glee,
In tiny moments, just be free!

A wink, a grin, a pun, a giggle,
Wrap it all in a silly jiggle.
Squeeze the day, don't let it slide,
On this wild, whimsical ride!

Less of the deep, more of the fun,
Life's a merry-go-round—run, run, run!
Take the mic, crack a joke,
Life's too short for the serious smoke.

Chase fleeting clouds, let nothing bore,
Savor the snacks, crave even more.
In quick-spun moments, find your spark,
Light up the world; make your mark!

Snapshots of the Soul

Life's like a camera, snap it quick,
Focus on joy, that's the trick.
Caught a grin, a silly pose,
Flip the script, let laughter flow.

Capture sunsets, capture smiles,
Flip your wig and dance for miles.
Moments flash like popcorn popped,
In life's theater, don't be stopped.

Shutter clicks, the world in view,
Tickled hearts and skies so blue.
A snapshot here, a giggle there,
Frame it all with a playful flair.

Keep it light, let the whimsy play,
Snap these moments, every day.
In snapshots bright, we find our role,
Life is funny, it snaps the whole!

Transient Truths of the Heart

In a fleeting moment, we giggle and sigh,
Chasing our shadows as minutes go by.
A spilled cup of coffee, a laugh in the air,
Reminds us of joy hidden everywhere.

We dance through the chaos, we stumble, we spin,
Finding our bliss in the mess that we're in.
With every sweet failure, a truth we unearth,
Life's not just a puzzle but a playful mirth.

With a wink and a nudge, we ponder the ride,
Bubbles of laughter, like sugar, collide.
Each hiccup of fate is a riddle to tease,
A circus of wonders; oh, life, if you please!

So here's to the moments that make spirits soar,
The transient truths that we can't help but adore.
In the blink of an eye, with a sigh and a cheer,
We toast to the whimsy that draws us all near.

Before the Clock Strikes

Tick-tock, tick-tock, the seconds cascade,
We're racing for insights, oh, what a charade!
With socks mispaired and hair askew,
We scramble for wisdom like kids in a zoo.

With a wink and a smile, we make sense of mess,
Concluding that life is a grand party dress.
We trip over thoughts and sometimes we fall,
Yet laughter arises, oh, isn't that all?

In this mad rush to figure it out,
We stumble through life with a giggle and shout.
Between bites of pizza and sips of cold brew,
We find bits of truth that are silly but true.

So raise up your glasses, and let's share a toast,
To the baffling moments we cherish the most.
Before the clock strikes, let's seize every beat,
Life's zest comes from laughter, oh, isn't that sweet?

A Breath Away from Insight

Pausing for breath, as the chaos subsides,
We find quirky wisdom in life's funny rides.
Like a game of charades where we mime with our hearts,
We fumble for meaning in the silliest parts.

The whispers of starlight, the giggles of fate,
All dance in the moments that we hesitate.
A sneeze during deep thoughts, a snort in the calm,
In the quirks of existence, we find soothing balm.

So when life feels heavy, just laugh it away,
Embrace all the madness, come what may!
For in every odd moment, a lesson's amiss,
A breath means our spirits can never dismiss.

In this fleeting journey where laughter ignites,
We're a breath away from pure, silly delights.
Catch the joy rolling in as it begins to unfold,
Life's secret's a belly laugh; that's what we're told.

Life's Secrets in Silhouettes

In the shadowplay of life, we grin and we glide,
Chasing our dreams with friends by our side.
Behind every silhouette, laughter's at play,
Whispering secrets in a chuckling way.

We jaunt through the dusk, with a skip and a hop,
Stumbling on truths that make our hearts stop.
Like silhouettes dancing, all awkward and free,
We ponder existence while sipping our tea.

Life's like a riddle, a puzzle we share,
With winks and with nudges, it's often quite rare.
We tumble through moments both silly and sweet,
Finding joy in the chaos, where crazy hearts meet.

So let's spin in the twilight, our laughter like gold,
Painting secrets in shadows, a story untold.
In the hues of the night, let your spirit take flight,
Life's a funny riddle, just embrace the delight.

Fleeting Glimpses of Reality

A cat on a roof, plotting its leap,
While I ponder my dreams, in a coffee cup deep.
Why do we chase after coins that we fold,
When happiness lives in the stories we're told?

A squirrel with a nut has his whole world in hand,
While I search for answers that slip like the sand.
In a dance with my shadow, I laugh at the sight,
As time tells its jokes in the soft morning light.

In the Blink of Wisdom

I asked a goldfish, 'What's great about life?'
It swam in circles, dodging my strife.
With fins full of wisdom, it swished and it swayed,
While I held my breath, wondering just what it said.

A man with a hat tried to sell me a dream,
But all that I got was a talking ice cream.
Yet fleeting the moments, they tickle the soul,
In the chaos of now, let's give laughter a roll.

What the Seconds Hold

In a tick of a clock, a pickle may dance,
As I munch on my snack, taking life with a chance.
Should I climb up a tree or just sit here and sing?
I'll laugh at the clouds, they're a whimsical thing.

Why worry about worries? They pile like old socks,
When laughter unravels, tick-tock, tick-tock.
With whimsy and chuckles, let time take a stroll,
For joy is the secret that fills up the bowl.

Spirited Insights in Short

A dog with a bone thinks it's king of the park,
While I ponder my fate, lost in thought, like a shark.
With squirrels as my audience, I'll take to the stage,
For comedy's grand, even on life's hardest page.

In fleeting exchanges, a smile can ignite,
Confetti in moments, that scatter delight.
With friends like the stars, we shine just as bright,
Let's dance through the chaos, and laugh into night.

The Essence of Now

In a world full of haste, we laugh and we play,
Chasing our shadows, we dance every day.
A coffee, a donut, the joy that we find,
Is tucked in those moments and shared with our kind.

With socks that don't match, we strut down the street,
Proclaiming our style is the one that's most neat.
Finding a penny brings luck for a while,
But laughter and friendship, now that's really style!

Life Unraveled in Instants

A sneeze in the quiet, a cat on the run,
Life's tangled moments can be quite the fun.
Catch the clock slipping, it's going too fast,
But with jokes in our pockets, we're having a blast!

We tumble and trip, yet we never lose cheer,
For each little blunder, there's laughter and beer.
So toast to the gaffes, they sparkle and shine,
Reminding us all that the jesters are fine!

Brief Detours on Infinite Roads

A wrong turn today can lead to a treat,
Like stumbling on snacks or a new kind of seat.
With every misstep, there's laughter to share,
As long as we wander, there's joy everywhere!

With paths made of giggles and detours of jest,
Life's scenic routes offer the very best quest.
So chuckle and wiggle, take the road less clear,
For the best little moments come free, my dear!

Parables in the Blink of an Eye

In a blink, there's a lesson, a smile, or a snack,
With humor and whimsy, we never look back.
Like a squirrel that forgets why it climbed that tall tree,
We bask in the goof, living wild and carefree.

A scoff at the serious, a wink at the grind,
In silliness found, a clear truth defined.
So let's raise a toast to the moments that fly,
For life is an echo, a laugh in the sky!

Epiphanies in an Hourglass

Time is like sand, it slips away,
Yet here I sit, in disarray.
Thoughts swirl 'round like a fun fair ride,
Questions answered? Just take it in stride.

A cat leaps by, it winks at me,
Does it know secrets of reality?
I ponder hard, then laugh out loud,
Life's just a joke, and I'm the crowd.

A sip of coffee, strong and hot,
Is this what wisdom's really got?
We float on bubbles; we sit on clouds,
Waving to the cosmic crowds.

Yet in this chaos, smiles ignite,
Finding joy in the absurd delight.
Let's dance with shadows, spin with cheer,
For life's too short; let's make it clear!

The Instant of Infinity

I caught a glimpse of the endless space,
A donut-shaped universe in a race.
Why did I think it'd all be plain?
Now, I'm just lost in a cosmic train.

Bright stars are winking, it's quite a scene,
Do they laugh at us, in our routine?
I asked a squirrel, it just chuckled back,
As it gathered nuts, I lost my track.

Time bends and twists like spaghetti in pots,
What IS reality? It ties us in knots.
A quirky thought, a bubble of air,
Life's just a joke, if we dare to share.

In moments of laughter, we find our way,
Through cosmic questions, we dance and sway.
So let's embrace the silly and wild,
In this grand joke, we're all just a child!

5 Minutes and Questions Unfold

With five minutes ticking, I ponder the fun,
What's the punchline? Are we ever done?
I flipped through pages of wise old books,
To find the meaning, in all the hooks.

A frog croaks loud, in the still of the night,
Is he pondering deep, or just taking flight?
I swear he's plotting—a comedic scheme,
To rule the pond and fulfill his dream.

With each tick-tock, my mind plays tricks,
Why is soup so good? Why do we fix?
A dance with absurdity fills the air,
As questions unite us—a quirky affair.

So grab a coffee, and let's debate,
Why do we laugh? Is it all just fate?
In five short minutes, we've cracked the code,
Life is a jest, let's lighten the load!

Moments of Revelation

In moments of silence, a thought did race,
Why are we here? Is it just for space?
I asked the bread if it felt like toast,
It crumbled softly, finding itself a host.

A bird swoops low, it gives me a glare,
Is it questioning life or just my hair?
I chuckle gently, it flaps away mad,
Even to birds, the answers look bad.

Conversations with waffles, and pie on a plate,
They've been around, but never too late.
Syrup drips sweet, like the wisdom we crave,
In laughter and chaos, we learn how to brave.

So here's to the giggles, the quirks, and the fun,
In the dance of existence, we all weigh a ton.
Let's toast to the moments, absurd and sublime,
For life is just humor, wrapped up in time!

The Paradox of Simplicity

In a world full of chaos, we seek the fun,
Simple joys slip by like a laugh on the run.
Counting clouds or juggling just a few,
Turns out the complex is more like a zoo.

Why ponder recipes or charts of all sorts,
When a pizza and a party bring all the reports?
We chase after wisdom like a squirrel in a tree,
But a good ol' joke is the best remedy.

Briefly, We Are

We stumble through life with a goofy grace,
Waving at moments that hummed and that raced.
Inquiries echo, but none seem quite right,
Except for that pizza on a Tuesday night.

We're here and we're gone like a flash in the pan,
Yet every weird mishap just adds to the plan.
Life's worth the giggles and hiccups we share,
With every quick chuckle, we lighten the air.

Life's Palette in a Blink

Colors spin wildly in this grand, silly show,
With each brush of the day, watch the giggles grow.
A dab of bright laughter, a splash of delight,
Mixing chaos and fun in the soft morning light.

From slapstick moments to tickles of fate,
The canvas of living is less about hate.
So grab a paintbrush, smear humor around,
And celebrate life where sheer joy can be found.

In the Twinkling of an Eye

In a blink, we exist, like a sneeze in the air,
Chasing our tails with a comical flair.
We hustle and bustle while tripping on shoe,
Yet giggles remind us it's just what we do.

Grab your rubber chicken, let's dance through the mess,
Life's playful parade is a glorious guess.
In the moments we giggle, the truth might just pry,
That wisdom is found in a joke and a pie.

Illuminated by a Flicker

A light bulb buzzes, bright and loud,
As thoughts dance dizzy, like a cloud.
Why chase the stars when snacks abound?
In chips and giggles, joy is found.

We ponder deep while on the loo,
With echoes of life, and fleeting view.
Is it cheese or wisdom that we seek?
Maybe both, with a side of peak!

A quirk of fate, a twist of fate,
In cosmic laughter, we celebrate.
What's with the fuss, the serious song?
Life's a sketch, we just tag along.

So grab your hat and dance a jig,
In silly hats, we feel so big.
With every fumble, the smiles bloom,
In a world of jokes, there's always room.

Parables of the Instant

In a blink, the coffee brews,
Philosophers intermingle with snooze.
Why ponder 'why' when 'how' is great?
Let's meditate on lunch, not fate!

Time flies fast, a comedian's jest,
Interrupts the wisdom we all quest.
Is success just pie in the sky?
Or simply a slice of pizza nearby?

Life's a buffet, take what you crave,
With mishaps and giggles, we're all brave.
Oh look! A squirrel in a tux!
Who needs the answers? Just enjoy the flux!

With jokes for breakfast, laughs for tea,
Life's a riddle, wild and free.
To seek enlightenment on roller skates,
Just twirl around, it never waits!

In Strokes of Time

Sketching moments with crayons bright,
In scribbles of laughter, day and night.
Why fret the canvas of our dreams?
When life's a laugh, or so it seems!

Tick-tock says the clock with glee,
It's not the lessons; it's the spree.
With jokes and friends, who needs a plan?
Just grab a snack, and take a stand!

In doodles of chaos, we find our way,
Adventures await, come what may.
Twisting and turning, like a dance,
Life's comedy, given a chance!

So laugh it off, let worries fade,
In server queues, a joke is made.
Life's an art, messy and clear,
With crayon hearts, we'll persevere!

Whirlwind of Wonders

In a whirl, we spin and twirl,
Chasing moments, oh what a whirl!
With rubber chickens and silly hats,
Life's a chuckle, where humor chats.

Zoom through time, no map in hand,
Contemplating why we can't just stand.
Is joy a dance or just a snack?
In every giggle, there's no lack!

We're surfing waves of blissful fun,
With mismatched socks under the sun.
So roll your eyes and take a leap,
Life's a circus—join the keep!

With every stumble, the spark ignites,
In laughter's arms, we find our heights.
So wave goodbye to reasons and doubt,
In a whirlwind of wonders, we shout!

Encapsulated Wisdom

In a world where time ticks fast,
We ponder truths that seldom last.
A cookie crumbles with sweet delight,
Is it wisdom? Oh, what a sight!

A selfie clicked, we pause to grin,
Chasing moments, we're in a spin.
Is that a sage or just my neighbor?
He laughs too hard; what's a sign of labor?

Life's a joke wrapped in a riddle,
Dance like a chicken, don't take it middle.
Pizza or salad, what should it be?
Flip a coin; that's how you see!

So here's the secret—easy and prime,
Life's absurd, but we make it rhyme.
With laughter echoing through the air,
Dance through the chaos without a care.

Life's Mirage in Moments

At dawn's first light, we sip our brews,
Contemplating if we should snooze.
A dash of chaos fills our day,
With mismatched socks—what can we say?

Tick-tock goes the clock, oh dear!
Let's race the cat—who has no fear.
An ice cream cone, a goofy smile,
Moments collect, let's bask awhile.

We chase our tails like dogs on runs,
With every misstep, laughter stuns.
The truth: we're all just passing through,
In this circus, we're the crew!

Life's a mirage, but oh so sweet,
With every tumble, it's still a treat.
Laugh out loud, it's pure delight,
Just hold on tight; embrace the flight!

An Instant to Awaken

A toast to those who wake with glee,
With pajamas worn, they drink their tea.
The toast pops up like a surprise,
Who knew breakfast would win the prize?

We chase our dreams like ducks in line,
Quacking schemes, we think we'll shine.
The cat just stretched—such bliss for him,
How do we reach that zen-filled whim?

A snapshot taken, faces absurd,
Life's a sitcom, haven't you heard?
With laughter echoes from door to door,
An instant crafted, we ask for more.

So grab your quirks, wear them like crowns,
In the royal court of ups and downs.
Awaken the silly, embrace the fun,
Life's silly dance has just begun!

Vignettes of Vitality

Life's a canvas all splashed with hue,
With scribbles that often debut.
One minute a whisper, the next a shout,
You question if you're missing out.

A frog jumps high, trying to croak,
Turns out, he's just telling a joke.
We stumble along, trip on a shoe,
In this comic routine, we find the true.

Puns and giggles are part of the game,
Each joy we capture has its own name.
Life's vignettes stitched with laughter bright,
Are reminders of what feels just right.

So slip on your shoes, with mismatched flair,
Join the parade of those who dare.
With hearts wide open, we'll ride this tide,
In life's funny journey, we take pride!

Life's Little Revelations

A cat knows all the secrets,
Whiskers twitching in delight.
Chasing shadows, missing lessons,
Yet naps under sunlight.

Coffee spills are deep insights,
Foamy lattes, tasty cues.
Frothy mustaches, silly faces,
Can lead to your next muse.

Walnuts fall from lofty branches,
Cracking laughs over the ground.
Squirrels dance in wild glances,
With wisdom not yet found.

So, gather all your giggles,
And share them with a friend.
Life's quirky little riddles,
Are truths that never end.

Countdown to Awareness

Tick-tock! The clock is laughing,
Time's a jester, full of tricks.
Feeling lost? Just start dancing,
And wear your rubber kicks.

Step one: acknowledge awkward,
Your two left feet have charm.
Memories may feel like chalkboard,
But wiggles will disarm.

Ask the goldfish what it thinks:
"Thoughts are bubbles in a bowl!"
Embrace the cringes and the kinks,
And keep your heart and soul.

With each countdown, heed the folly,
Three seconds to unwind your mind.
In laughter, don't be too coy,
Just enjoy what you can find.

One Breath, Infinite Realizations

Inhale deep, release that giggle,
Life's a balloon set to pop.
Catch those dreams before they wiggle,
And send them high with a hop.

Each breath a mini-vacation,
Airplanes are made of smiles.
Riding clouds of innovation,
At least for a little while.

Bleeps and blunders make it spicy,
Mistakes are just fancy art.
So when it gets too dicey,
Slap on a grin, play smart.

As the moment drifts like mist,
Breathe it in; there's much to gain.
Make a wish, you might be kissed,
By all the laughter in the rain.

Transient Truths

Fleeting moments, winks of fate,
Like socks that disappear.
Chase the humor; don't be late,
Laughter's always near.

Silly ducks and crooked paths,
Life's a game of tag.
Dance like nobody's watching,
While wearing your best rag.

Coffee stains are life's confessions,
Spilled stories on the page.
Finding wisdom in transgressions,
And humor in the age.

Time to toast with plastic cups,
To meaning muddied in a whirl.
Just remember to fill it up,
And let joy be your pearl.

Time's Subtle Messages

Tick tock goes the clock,
Time waits for no one,
Yet here I sit and snack,
Why is this so much fun?

Messages from the stars,
Like emails from my mom,
"Don't forget the car,
Also, vacuum your home!"

Life's a jigsaw puzzle,
With edge pieces mismatched,
I guess I'll make it work,
Or just buy a new batch!

Each second's a treasure,
A chance to try and cheer,
So bring out the confetti,
And maybe a cold beer!

Epiphany in the Now

Sitting here in silence,
What's life's great secret?
A thought just came to me,
Hey, wait! I lost my feet.

Carrots, cupcakes, and dreams,
They swirl in a dance,
Stumbling over my schemes,
But hey, isn't it a chance?

Coffee helps me ponder,
Or is it just the cream?
Epiphanies grow fonder,
While I drift from my dream.

In minutes filled with laughter,
Life's meaning's like a game,
Play it with joy thereafter,
What's your favorite name?

Moments that Define Us

A heart shaped like a muffin,
What does it convey?
Maybe to keep stuffing,
With frosting every day!

Moments flash like lightning,
Quick thoughts that start to glow,
Do I move or start writing?
Must I be a star in a show?

Dancing in the kitchen,
Who knew that's a skill?
Fumbling, though I'm pitching,
A recipe for thrill!

Defining each small moment,
With laughter in the air,
Life's puzzle is component,
Working like a fresh hair.

Hidden Wonders of the Minute

In every tick of time,
A giggle lurks inside,
With chaos and with rhyme,
Come join the silly ride!

Dandelions take their stand,
In cracks of pavement brown,
Are we not all just sand?
Or heroes in a gown?

Minute mysteries abound,
Like ketchup on a pie,
Keep searching all around,
And ponder every why!

So here's to the quirky,
In all that we can find,
Hidden wonders, oh so murky,
Just laughter, here, aligned!

Life in a Flash

In a blink, we race ahead,
Chasing dreams, or maybe bread.
Tick-tock goes the clock's parade,
What's that? A snack? I'm unafraid!

A wink, a laugh, a sly little joke,
These moments shine, like bright oak smoke.
Life's simple zest, just add some spice,
And of course, don't forget the rice!

Skimming stones on a pond of thought,
Sometimes lessons can't be bought.
Dance like no one seems to care,
But watch out for that guy with the chair!

So raise a toast to the quick and sly,
For in a flash, we learn to fly.
Lament not lost seconds in fright,
Embrace the goofy, embrace the light.

Heartbeats of Understanding

Lost in thought beneath the sun,
We ponder life—a race, a run.
But is it much more than a dash?
Let's take a break, share a laugh, and splash!

Feel the rhythm of a heart that beats,
In this journey, oh so sweet.
A coffee spill? A slight delay,
Sometimes that's the best part of the day!

Questions swirl like leaves in fall,
What's the meaning? Beats us all!
Yet a wink shared with a stranger's grin,
Reminds us where understanding begins.

So grab a snack, let's not be shy,
In every heartbeat, just give it a try.
Connecting pieces in a hasty dance,
Life's so funny; we must take a chance.

Passing Thoughts

Thoughts like butterflies take flight,
Flitting by in sheer delight.
One lands soft upon my nose,
"Did you pay the bills?" it almost blows!

Colors flash in memory's game,
Each silly moment, none the same.
Got an errand? Write it down,
Or forget—just wear that frown!

To ponder deep or swim the stream,
As life unfolds, it's all a dream.
But what's that? A snack or treat?
Hold on—can we rewind to repeat?

So wave goodbye to passing thoughts,
Find joy in blunders, laugh a lot!
In life's swift surf, let's take the ride,
With humor as our loyal guide.

Lasting Impact

With every joke that hits the spot,
We crinkle up, forget what's hot.
A friend's wide grin, a share of fries,
That's the secret, hear the wise!

Funny faces, the silliest sound,
In these moments, joy is found.
For laughter sticks, it makes a mark,
Likes little fireflies in the dark.

Life's less about the heavy things,
And more about the joy it brings.
So let's not sweat the little woes,
Wear flip-flops, dance like it shows!

A lasting impact, light and free,
Just take a step, come laugh with me.
In each quick moment, capture the gift,
Grab the slice, let laughter drift!

A Moment's Clarity

In a moment, all seems clear,
Like a vending machine with root beer.
Life's puzzles present a quirky twist,
Don't just ponder, grab a fist!

A colorful cast of characters leap,
Here's wisdom hidden, a secret to keep.
Look closer now, beneath the laugh,
Clarity rests just like a photograph.

Do we chase riches or choose to roam?
A nap, a plan, or just go home?
Sticky notes in wild disarray,
Living clumsily—hey, that's okay!

A moment's clarity can sneak up high,
With laughter echoing, you'll surely fly.
So dance with joy, let silliness stay,
Life's a wild ride, come what may!

The Brief Journey Within

I took a trip inside my head,
With snacks and thoughts to share instead.
The paths were twisty, oh so odd,
A map, I guess, is quite a fraud.

In search of wisdom, I did roam,
Found a sock and called it home.
The questions swirled like candy floss,
But answers? Well, they took a loss.

Chasing sunsets at breakneck speed,
My brain just giggled, it's a weed.
With every tick and tock I sought,
A meaning hidden, but I forgot.

In five short minutes, I conclude,
Life's just a game and I'm the dude.
With laughter echoing through the void,
I'll wear this bliss, no need to avoid.

Seconds of Solace

In a world that spins so fast,
I paused to ponder, but it passed.
A twinkle in my eye did glare,
'Why worry?' said my comfy chair.

I brewed a cup, I settled down,
Through fleeting minutes wearing a frown.
Then suddenly, I spilled my tea,
A mess was life, oh silly me!

I made a list, then lost the pen,
Recalled a dog named 'Fluffykins.'
A worm danced by, I waved hello,
It smiled back, and stole the show.

So here I am, with wisdom's grace,
Embracing chaos at my pace.
In seconds found, a fleeting thrill,
Life's punchline is a hearty chill.

The Tapestry of Moments

A tapestry of silly threads,
Woven tight with laughs and shreds.
Each moment stitched with love and quirk,
I sometimes wonder, 'What's the jerk?'

A cat just jumped and stole my seat,
I laughed aloud, can't feel my feet.
With every stitch, a giggle shared,
I realize life is lightly spared.

I twirled around like a cotton ball,
Embracing nonsense, I feel tall.
An artful blend of joy and blunder,
Like lightning bolts of fun and thunder.

So take a look at life's design,
It's filled with chocolate, quite divine.
In every mess and every cheer,
The art of living draws us near.

Whispers of the Timeless

In whispers soft like cotton candy,
Time shared tricks, both light and dandy.
If clocks could talk, they'd make you chuckle,
For seconds tick in goofy struggle.

An hourglass turned into a squirrel,
It spun around, oh what a whirl!
With every tick, a joke they told,
The wisdom wrapped in jokes of old.

I danced with past and future too,
In wobbly steps, like kangaroo.
Each moment laughed, and sang a tune,
Life's like a wacky balloon.

So, here's to time that bends and sways,
To silly paths and laugh-filled days.
In every tick, a gift so prime,
Life's just a wink, a laugh, a rhyme.

The Instants that Illuminate

In a blink, we laugh and play,
Chasing thoughts that slip away.
With a grin, we grab the day,
Thinking, 'Is this what they say?'

Sipping coffee, spilling dreams,
Life's a puzzle, or so it seems.
With each giggle, reality beams,
Turning woes to sunny themes.

Juggling tasks, a circus show,
When did time decide to go slow?
We dance on toes, with faces aglow,
Winking at sunsets, putting on a rodeo.

So here we stand, poised to dare,
Grinning wide, without a care.
In these moments, we're almost where
Life's absurdity fills the air.

Quick Visions of Our Journey

Zooming through life's crazy ride,
Each twist a giggle, each turn a slide.
We pack our bags with ease and pride,
But forget our snacks, oh what a stride!

Scribbled notes on napkins found,
Dreams and wishes, tightly wound.
"Beep beep!" we hear, a joyful sound,
The universe laughs, in joy profound.

So in a flash, we see our fate,
A buffet line where we all plate.
Life's buffet is worth the wait,
If you can feast before the gate!

With each moment, a shade of fun,
Here's the punchline, the best one:
In silly chaos, we often run,
Discovering joy, we've already won!

Ever-changing Narratives of Now

In a whisper, fate will unfold,
Each tale a quirk, each laugh bold.
Reality's fabric, in hand we hold,
As we journey, oh so uncontrolled.

Sticky notes with dreams in light,
Wishing for courage, taking flight.
"Oops!" we say, in day or night,
Stumbling through with sheer delight.

Pause the clock, take a chance,
Let's unite in this silly dance.
Unearth the truth, enhance the romance,
A gaggle of giggles in life's expanse.

Moments, like bubbles, in the air,
Floating gently, beyond compare.
Life is a stage and we're aware,
That laughter is the best affair!

Stolen Moments of Truth

A coffee spill, a moment rare,
Truth unveiled in playful glare.
We find meaning in messy hair,
Rolling laughter beyond compare.

Quick winks shared on crowded streets,
With banter light, our joy repeats.
Under the chaos, fun teems,
Truth resides in laughter's gleams.

A stumble here, a loaf of bread,
In absurdity, humor is spread.
With every mishap, we're better fed,
Stories grow, forever widespread.

So let us pause in this rib-tickling spree,
Grab hold of laughter, let it be free.
In silly moments, we find jubilee,
With stolen truths that set us glee.

Brief Sparks of Clarity

In a jar of pickles, a light bulb glows,
Searching for wisdom where no one goes.
A cat takes a nap, the world's unrest,
Maybe naps are the key to success.

Why chase rainbows with pots of gold?
When socks in the dryer tell tales untold.
Life's a riddle painted in bright hues,
Simple solutions often wear clown shoes.

Time's Gentle Revelations

A sandwich lost in the fridge's abyss,
Gives lessons on love, like a soft, chewy kiss.
The clock ticks loudly, yet whispers so sweet,
Time has a way to make chaos feel neat.

A sneeze at the wrong time can cause much confusion,
Yet laughter erupts, it's a comical fusion.
From crumbs on the counter to dreams taking flight,
Revealing life's truths in the soft morning light.

An Instant of Insight

A rubber chicken dons a scholar's cap,
With puns and giggles, it maps out a gap.
Why not dance in the rain on a Tuesday night?
Life's heavy questions need laughter to take flight.

A fortune cookie speaks with spicy delight,
"Skip the deep thoughts, just hold the kite tight."
Moments of clarity wrapped in a pun,
Leave us chuckling, like children who run.

In a Minute, the Universe

From waffle iron dreams to toast in the sky,
The universe chuckles as mornings slip by.
Time flies with the zeal of a puppy at play,
Leading us to answers in its own quirky way.

A butterfly lands on a stack of old books,
It whispers sweet wisdom with shimmering looks.
In chaos and laughter, life finds its groove,
The universe winks; it's all one big move.

Life in the Fast Lane

A squirrel with a helmet speeds past on his bike,
Chasing his dreams with a pep and a hike.
In life's little moments, we learn to be bold,
Finding joy in the simple, the quirky, the gold.

Jumping in puddles, the best form of skill,
Finding answers in laughter, what a delightful thrill.
When time offers lessons, it's fun to play,
In a wild, zany dance, we find our own way.

Perspectives Born from Seconds

Tick-tock, the clock's a tease,
Rushing thoughts like buzzing bees.
Count your blessings, not your woes,
Dance like nobody knows.

In a bubble of fleeting time,
Forget the mountain, chase the climb.
Grab a snack, share a smile,
Life's a carnival, stay awhile!

The Briefest Of Contemplations

Take a break, enjoy the sun,
Silly faces, just for fun!
Jokes and laughter fill the air,
In this chaos, we find flair.

Wisdom found in pizza slices,
Life's a game, toss out the spices.
Silly hats and quirky shoes,
It's a ride, no time for blues!

Life Reduced to a Breath

Breathe in deep, exhale the stress,
Moments stacked can be a mess.
Brief encounters, quirky charms,
Hold your loved ones in your arms.

Laughter bubbles, fear like fluff,
Life's a game; it's never rough.
Wear a smile, let joy be free,
Who needs plans? Just let it be!

Glimmers of Revelation

Sudden thoughts, like popcorn pop,
Meaning's found right at the stop.
Chase your dreams with all your might,
In the dark, be your own light.

Frogs and toads, they croak and cheer,
Let's celebrate, bring on the beer!
Life's a puzzle, pieces flip,
Grab your friends, enjoy the trip!

Seconds to Salvation

In a café, I sip my brew,
Life's deep secrets, just a view.
Brows furrowed, I ponder hard,
Then spill my coffee, oh how marred!

With every tick, the moments flee,
Laughing at fate, it's just so free.
A joke repeats, like echoes loud,
I smile, realizing I'm quite proud.

The clock strikes noon, I nibble pie,
Wonder if squirrels might fly high.
A riddle dances on my plate,
What is life? A pastry fate!

In seconds gone, I seek to glean,
A comical twist in the routine.
Life's a comedy, just leave out strife,
Grab the giggles; that's the life!

Captured Insights

In the mirror, I see my face,
Wonder if I'm winning this race.
A sock on my foot, but where's the pair?
Is that wisdom or just despair?

Chasing dreams like runaway cats,
They pounce on my thoughts, where are my mats?
I shout to the universe, loud and clear,
It chuckles back, "Oh dear, oh dear!"

A spoonful of laughter feeds the soul,
While popcorn kernels dance and roll.
Understanding's a marvelous jest,
Just try not to keep it all compressed!

Captured moments, they slip away,
I'm left with puns in bright array.
The secret's out, so clap your hands,
Life's a silly game with rhyming bands!

Snapshots of Understanding

I take a snap, the world's in sight,
Wonders abound, both day and night.
Captured grins, those happy things,
Like cats in hats, oh what it brings!

Each snapshot tells a silly tale,
Of dancing ducks and a dog with braille.
Happiness flickers, then it's gone,
Like a fridge magnet's absurd brawn.

Life's a circus on a tiny thread,
With clowns and laughter all widespread.
I pause and giggle at the absurd,
Finding wisdom without a word.

Moments fly, like leaves in air,
So to the wild, I'll always dare.
With snapshots treasured on my phone,
I capture joy while feeling grown!

Grains of Time

Grains of sand slip through my hands,
Life's funny little, fleeting strands.
Tickling toes in an empty beach,
Philosophy's out of my reach.

I clamber up, while seagulls squawk,
Thoughts run wild as I take a walk.
Is this the truth? Do I know less?
My only wisdom? Wear clean dress!

Counting grains, I ponder fast,
Why does it feel like it's a blast?
The sun dips low, I strike a pose,
A selfie with laughter—let's all compose!

So here's the key, if I may boast,
Life's a party, so raise a toast!
Embrace the silly, dance with glee,
For joy is the answer, clearly!

Pearls of Wisdom

Pearls of wisdom, strung on a line,
Like jellybeans, they spark and shine.
Each shiny orb, a giggle tale,
With unexpected twists that never fail.

Sipping tea with a wisdom snail,
Tells me secrets of the grand trail.
"Life's a noodle, long and bent,
Just hang on tight, it's time well spent."

A slapstick punchline in the air,
Tickles my ribs, banishes care.
I trip and laugh, get back on track,
This cosmic joke? I'll never lack!

So pearls and laughter intertwine,
Life's a riddle, sparkly, divine!
In every chuckle, truth does hide,
So wear your smile with a tuxedo guide!

The Art of Brief Reflection

In a world so vast and wide,
We ponder deep, but then reside.
Life's questions swirl like autumn leaves,
Yet laughter brings us sweet reprieves.

A sock may vanish, chocolates melt,
Mysteries in life that we've all felt.
When chaos calls and plans go awry,
Just dance a jig, let worries fly!

We chase after answers, big and small,
But sometimes joy's the greatest call.
A playful wink, or puppy's bark,
Shows us where we leave our mark.

So gather round, friends, for a toast,
To fleeting moments we cherish most.
With humor's grace, we find our way,
And laugh at life, come what may.

Time's Subtle Lessons

Life's a riddle, wrapped in fun,
A puzzle game we've all but won.
With hiccups here and giggles there,
Time teaches us without a care.

The clock keeps ticking, loud it seems,
As we chase after silly dreams.
A cat nap here, a snack or two,
It's okay to skip a thing or few.

In moments rushed and seconds fled,
A silent giggle's often bred.
So check your watch, then toss it away,
Let whimsy lead the dance today!

For as we laugh, we learn to cope,
With frolicking hearts and loads of hope.
Here's to the absurd and the sweet embrace,
Life's not a race—it's a playful space!

Quick Flickers of Truth

Blink and you'll miss the secret key,
Life's brief lessons float like debris.
A swipe of luck, a dash of fate,
Understanding comes, but not too late.

When life gives you lemons, make a pie,
Or wear them like hats—give it a try!
The trick is knowing when to jest,
In laughter, truly, we are blessed.

A sandwich dropped, a spilled drink,
Fleeting moments make us rethink.
With every blunder, a light bulb glows,
In fleeting joy, true wisdom shows.

So take those slips and wear them proud,
Join in the ruckus, be bold, be loud!
For life's a comic strip, drawn in haste,
Each misstep adds to the wondrous taste.

A Sip of Wisdom

Pour a cup of jests today,
Sip the humor, let it play.
A sprinkle of wit, a dash of fun,
In quirky moments, wisdom's spun.

Why worry 'bout the things unseen?
Embrace the goofy, love the in-between.
A wink, a grin, a tickling joke,
In silliness, life's smoke is broke.

A tiny dance in chairs so small,
Remember, folks, we're here to ball.
So jump around, shake off the blues,
For joy's a sip—take a big cruise!

When searching for gold in days so wild,
Laugh like a kid, be carefree and mild.
Life's treasure shines in each chuckling sound,
In every heartbeat, true joy is found!

The Art of Living Now

Grab your snack, take a seat,
Life's a game, not a feat.
Dance like no one's in sight,
Laugh 'til it feels just right.

Chase the sun, or catch a breeze,
Talk to plants if you please.
Sing out loud, don't hold back,
Life's a joy, don't fade to black.

Count your blessings, share a grin,
Pet a dog and let them in.
Joke with friends, embrace the quake,
Life's a show, for goodness' sake!

Forget your woes, enjoy the zest,
Every moment's a silly fest.
Take a breath, it's time to play,
Live it up, both night and day.

Seconds to Serenity

In a flurry, find your bliss,
Take a break, not a miss.
Count your laughs, one by one,
Jump and shout, let's have some fun!

Stare at clouds, make a face,
Life's a carnival, join the race.
Dance with shadows, chase the light,
Life's absurd, embrace the fright.

Sit on grass, wiggle your toes,
Sniff some flowers, strike a pose.
Take a sip of lemonade,
Let your worries slowly fade.

Skate on puddles, laugh like kids,
Life's a treasure trove of jibs.
Every second's a laughing twist,
Live it up, you get the gist!

A Snapshot of Significance

Snap a photo, strike a pose,
Life's a giggle, goodness knows.
Capture joy, let sorrows slide,
In this moment, take a ride.

Doodle dreams, let colors swirl,
Life's an adventure, give it a whirl.
Eat dessert before the meal,
In this chaos, find the peel.

Whistle tunes, invent a song,
Life's a journey, won't be long.
Zoom through moments, grab a bite,
Spoon-fed wisdom, hold on tight.

Chase the quirks, let laughter ring,
Life's a giggle, it's a fling.
Celebrate the silly, it's your turn,
In this heartbeat, brightly burn.

Moments of True Awareness

Wake and wonder, what's the fuss?
Life's a circus, ride the bus.
Breathe in deep, imagine wide,
Take the ride, don't hide inside.

Balance fun on a hairy wire,
Light the candle, fuel your fire.
Find the bliss in everyday,
Silly games in silly play.

Tickle time, don't take it slow,
Life's a dance, so let it flow.
Splash in puddles, kiss the sky,
Life's a giggle, give it a try.

Moments flit like butterflies,
Seek the funny, win the prize.
Enjoy the ride, it's never plain,
Life's a canvas, stain the grain.

Life's Essence in a Glimpse

Wake up, the sun is bright,
Coffee spills, what a sight!
Chasing dreams on a busy road,
But sometimes, it's just a toad.

Laugh and dance in your own way,
Wear mismatched socks for the day!
Life's a joke that's worth the fling,
And don't forget to laugh and sing!

Find the joy in silly things,
Like a dog chasing after strings.
Embrace the weird, let chaos reign,
Because normal feels a bit mundane.

So live your life, don't take a pause,
Even if it sometimes gives you flaws.
Life's short, and that much is true,
Just eat that cake, let your heart renew.

Transitory Thoughts on Infinity

Count the stars with one quick glance,
Why is everyone in a hurry to dance?
Time's a thief, or so they claim,
I'd rather play a quirky game!

Infinity feels like a long meme,
Are we just flowers in a sunbeam?
Life's a circus, grab a seat,
Balance on one leg, that's quite a feat!

What's the rush to figure it all?
All you need is a good chuckle and a ball.
So trip over thoughts, don't lose the fun,
Life's a wacky rollercoaster run!

When in doubt, just take a leap,
Embrace the chaos, don't lose sleep.
With laughter echoing all around,
You'll find your peace, lost and found.

A Minute's Mandate

In a minute, you might just grin,
Understanding life's a playful spin.
Why worry 'bout what's in the cards?
Instead, let's play hopscotch in the yards.

A giggle here, a chuckle there,
Connecting laughter is our best affair.
Worry less about the grand plan,
Dance like a dog, oh what a span!

Coffee breaks and silly chats,
Life's more fun with friendly spats.
Each moment's a chance to just be kind,
And leave the heavy thoughts behind.

So let's embrace the silly ride,
With humor as our trusty guide.
Just remember, when times get rough,
A hearty laugh is really enough!

Light Bulbs of Perception

Switch it on, let's have a laugh,
Life's a quirky, easy half.
Dance with light bulbs, twirl and sway,
Life is precious, come what may!

Why chase shadows, when it's bright?
Mix up your choices, ignite the night.
A joke here, a pun there,
Illuminating life isn't so rare!

Funny hats and mismatched shoes,
Let's paint the world in vibrant hues.
Take a moment, look around,
You might just find where joy is found!

Life's a flicker, bright and bold,
Chase that light, let stories unfold.
So grab a friend, and let's be silly,
Because life, my friend, is meant to be frilly!

Life's Essence in a Moment

We run in circles, that's our game,
Chasing our tails, isn't it a shame?
With coffee cups and late-night snacks,
We ponder deep while watching our backs.

A squirrel mocks us from a tree,
It's probably wiser, would you agree?
While we debate our cosmic plight,
He just gathers nuts, oh what a sight!

A post-it note with dreams so grand,
Yet here we sit with snacks in hand.
The universe laughs as we bite down,
On donuts and whims, we spin round and round.

So here's my cue to laugh and run,
Life's just a joke, let's have some fun!
So raise a glass to the silly chase,
And dance with glee in this wild space.

Beyond Time's Embrace

In the clock's tick, we find our beat,
Yet we stumble on our own two feet.
Counting down like it's a race,
When frozen yogurt is still in place.

A fleeting thought like a soap bubble,
Pops in our head amid the hubble.
"Why are we here?" we loudly cry,
As the cat yawns and winks an eye.

Sandcastles built with dreams so bright,
Wash away with the incoming tide.
But we'll just build another, on a whim,
Even as the horizon starts to dim.

So cheers to the chaos, wild and free,
Life's a buffet, come eat with me!
With laughter we'll ride this cosmic wave,
For in the absurd, we all must brave.

Quick Reflections on Being

A toaster pops, and we jump in fright,
Did we really come from stardust light?
Or just breakfast crumbs on a Sunday morn,
Peeking through life, slightly worn.

In the midst of chaos, we breathe and sigh,
As socks disappear, oh my, oh my!
Is purpose found in the laundry pile?
Or is it in laughter that makes us smile?

Frogs leap by with existential woes,
They croak profound thoughts nobody knows.
We chuckle and joke, while sipping our tea,
Finding wisdom in oddity, just you and me.

Let's not fret about grand designs,
Life's little quirks are what truly shines.
With giggles and joys, our hearts find their place,
In this short dance through time and space.

Ephemeral Echoes of Purpose

A fleeting thought, like a butterfly,
I grasp too late as it flits on by.
In coffee shops, we ponder and muse,
While life outside bakes in the sun's dues.

Ducklings waddle as we sip our lattes,
Chasing crumbs and searching for parties.
"Are we awake?" someone shouts with glee,
As a pigeon scoffs, "Just look at me!"

Plans on napkins, ideas on a whim,
Yet trip over what's real, how quaint and grim.
Life is a circus, with clowns and jest,
Take a deep breath, in laughter, invest.

So let's raise our glasses to folly and cheer,
And toast to the moments we hold so dear.
For in this parade of the odd and the bright,
We find joy in the chaos, our own little light.

Ephemeral Whispers

A cat sneezes, time slips wide,
Chasing shadows we can't abide.
Jellybeans and silly hats,
Wisdom shared with quirky cats.

Tick-tock sings the clock of dreams,
Bubblegum and silly schemes.
Dance like the stars are just for you,
Grab a giggle, through and through.

Life's a movie with comic breaks,
A mishap with frosted cakes.
Punchlines land, then run away,
We laugh and stumble through the fray.

In the end, it's just a jest,
Perhaps a nap is what is best.
So take a breath, enjoy the ride,
With a wink and chuckle, slide with pride.

A Stopwatch of Existence

A stopwatch ticking, what a tease,
Counting laughs and little wheezes.
Banana peels and tumbleweeds,
Life's a joke, it often leads.

Grab your snacks and hold on tight,
Hiccups challenge the moonlight.
Running in circles, who's in charge?
Behind the scenes, it's all just large.

Tickle your fate with a rubber chicken,
While noodles dance, and clocks are stricken.
Memories bounce like ping-pong balls,
Joy erupts at life's wild calls.

So as time winks, don't take it grave,
Jump on the train, be merry and brave.
In this madcap ride, just smile and sing,
Life's a party, so let's all swing!

Blink and Understand

In a blink, the cake's all gone,
Where did the time run off and spawn?
Flip a pancake, right side up,
Celebrate it all with a crazy cup.

Clouds giggle as raindrops play,
A cat in pajamas cheers the day.
Chasing ducks in a hurry, oh!
Stop and ponder, then let it go.

Wisdom hides in pizza crusts,
Among the gooey, cheesy musts.
Each slice tells tales of sweet surprise,
Like joy in a talk with wise old fries.

What's the secret? Who can say?
Embrace the chuckles along the way.
In joyful chaos, we live our fate,
With a wink, and then we celebrate!

Fleeting Moments of Clarity

Life's a riddle wrapped in cheese,
Tickle your toes in a summer breeze.
Balloons float and dreams take flight,
Spotting a unicorn in plain sight.

Pineapple on pizza? Absolute bliss,
Finding joy in every twist and kiss.
Dance on ceilings, jump on walls,
Embrace the echoes in silly calls.

Time's a lemonade, sweet and tart,
Sip it slowly, use your heart.
With bubble wands and tricks up sleeves,
Life's a circus, filled with leaves.

So embrace the giggle, chase the fun,
In the grand parade, join everyone.
The clock won't wait, so hold on tight,
Time's silly chase, is pure delight!

Minutes Unveiled

A cat lays sprawled across the floor,
Dreams of fish and sun, nothing more.
In a world that spins, he's got the knack,
Five blissful minutes, no time to lack.

The clock ticks loud, but he does not care,
He chases shadows; what's life? A dare.
With each little pounce, he finds his bliss,
In moments like these, who needs to miss?

A splash of milk and a ball of string,
Who knew such joy could come from a fling?
Forget the cosmos, the stars, the way,
For feline antics, I'll gladly stay.

So here's to laughter, to joy, to fun,
Life's silly moments must weigh a ton.
In five short ticks, the truth may unfurl,
Just roll with the punches, dance in a whirl.

The Pulse of Now

A squirrel dashes, all twitch and tail,
Hoarding acorns, he's ready to sail.
Each nut's a treasure, each chase a thrill,
In the game of life, he's got the skill.

Why waste the time on heavy debates?
The secret of joy? Just eat your crates.
With each nut stored, he twirls with glee,
Life's simple pleasures are key, just see!

Coffee spills and a messy room,
With laughter and joy, there's plenty of room.
We dance through the chaos, the spills and the sweeps,
All as the clock quietly ticks and keeps.

So laugh at the mishaps and cherish the now,
For moments like these? You'll never have brow.
In funny little tales, let's find our bliss,
Where life's pulse beats strong, wrapped in a kiss.

Fleeting Thoughts on What Matters

A bird takes flight, then lands with a hop,
Chasing breadcrumbs, he'll never stop.
In search of snacks, he knows no failure,
With chipmunk buddies, he'll be the tailor.

They plan their feasts, with giggles and cheer,
No grand philosophies; it's all crystal clear.
In fleeting moments, friendships bloom bright,
The snack of joy is the greatest delight.

Life is a banquet, a buffet of fun,
With jellybeans tossed, there's nowhere to run.
So let's be like birds, free and light,
With silly adventures that soar out of sight.

For in the end, with each nibble and cheer,
We find that joy's close, always near.
Through laughter and snacks, it's plain to see,
Life's richest feast is where you're just free.

A Whisper from Tomorrow

A turtle wanders, slow and steady,
In the midst of chaos, he is ready.
Each step he takes, a thought or two,
Life's a stroll, not a hurried view.

In whimsical whims, he ponders the day,
With dreams of seaweed and sun's warm ray.
"Why rush," he says, with a cheerful grin,
Life's a race? Nah, let the laughter begin.

With each little rock and shade that he finds,
He gathers good vibes, like butterfly minds.
In five sweet minutes, he'll rule the shore,
While thoughts of tomorrow just constantly soar.

So let us wander, slow and bold,
In the joyful moments that never get old.
With turtles as mentors, we sing our tune,
Life's about fun, like songs to the moon!

The Flash of Existence

In a blink, we come and go,
With socks that never match, you know.
We laugh, we cry, then it's time to play,
Why does the cat think it's a buffet?

Chasing dreams like wild balloons,
While eating cakes and hummus spoons.
Life's a game of hide and seek,
But who's hiding? It's often the week!

We dance like no one cares to see,
In our pajamas, just you and me.
Moments come, tick-tock, they flee,
Wait—did I really just eat that pea?

So grab your friends and make a fuss,
We'll talk nonsense, just for us.
In a flash, it's all a jest,
Embrace the chaos, that's the best!

Quickfire Musings

Tickle your toes and hum a tune,
Life is short—don't waste it, moon!
We giggle at the big and small,
Like trying to fit in that blue overalls.

Time is a man with an empty plate,
He'll rush through dinner, forget the cake.
But who needs dessert? Oh, wait, we do!
There's always room for one more chew!

Fleeting thoughts in a busy head,
Like shoes misplaced beneath the bed.
Another day, and where's my shoe?
Life's a circus, and you're the zoo!

With quirky friends and silly plans,
We often forget how much life can span.
So here's a toast, raise your cups,
To loving life, and to all the pups!

Whispers of Existence

In the quiet, we hear a laugh,
Just a whisper—like a photograph.
We chase the sun and paint the sky,
But wait, did I just lose my tie?

Life's a puzzle, we play the game,
Collecting quirks, not just fame.
So what if tomorrow is a mess?
We'll wear mismatched shoes, nonetheless!

The clock says hurry, but I say chill,
Let's ponder life on a spinning wheel.
With every tick, the absurd we find,
Is that a cat, or did I just rewind?

In a world of chaos, make it bright,
Laugh at the shadows, dance in the light.
So here's to fun—and silly dreams,
Life's more vibrant than it seems!

Fleeting Seconds of Wonder

Time zips by like a runaway train,
But we're still here, a bit insane.
With ice cream splatters on our shirts,
We ponder questions with jazzy flirts.

Like where are my keys? And where's my hat?
Life's a riddle wrapped in a cat.
We giggle as we chase the breeze,
And check if we remembered to sneeze.

Moments glimmer, they twist and spin,
Like the stories told with a cheeky grin.
So stand up, dance, and let it flow,
Life's a party—this much we know!

Raise a toast for the quickened pace,
To laughter and joy, let's embrace.
In these fleeting seconds, just have fun,
We're all just stardust, and we've just begun!

The Clock Strikes Insight

Tick-tock goes the clock,
What's the secret? Not quite shock.
A sandwich, a joke, a quick drink,
Life isn't deep, just make it stink.

Don't ponder long, or you might trip,
On the meaning you'll gladly skip.
Jump on the train of silly dreams,
Leave the heavy stuff to screams.

In a rush? Just laugh and grin,
Who cares if you lose or win?
Grab your shoes, let's dance about,
Life's short, let's laugh and shout.

Right now's the time, so don't delay,
Embrace the chaos, come what may.
With wit and whimsy we shall thrive,
In five minutes, feel alive!

Brevity of Being

Why do we fret with such concern?
Life's a dance, so take a turn.
A joke, a pun, a sight to see,
In the end, it's all just glee.

Skip the drama, let's take a ride,
On the rollercoaster of your pride.
Forget the quest for deep "aha!"
Grab a cupcake, and voila!

With every tick, find joy and cheer,
Life's a party, my dear.
Spaghetti flies and pie in the face,
Time flies in this joyous race.

So raise a toast to every blunder,
With laughter loud and pure wonder.
In the briefest moments that we cling,
Find the fun in everything!

Enlightenment in a Heartbeat

Just a heartbeat, that's the key,
Why so serious? Just let it be.
Knock-knock jokes and silly puns,
In this life, we're all just funs!

Life's a buffet, grab what you like,
I'll take the laughter, you take the hike.
Forget the worries, bring the treats,
In joy, life's flavor truly beats.

So if you ponder what's the deal,
Just laugh a lot, that's the appeal.
In five minutes, we'll find our bliss,
With every giggle, we'll reminisce.

So let's set sail on this crazy ride,
With humor as our trusty guide.
In the heartbeat, we find delight,
In every corner, day or night.

Seconds of Serenity

A second here, a giggle there,
Why take life with such a care?
Bubbles, balloons, a silly hat,
In this circus, we all just chat.

Take a breath, don't hold it tight,
Just dance your way into the light.
The secret's not in deep despair,
It's in the cupcakes you can share!

Grab your friends for a joyful spree,
Laugh till it hurts, just wait and see.
A wink, a nudge, it's all a game,
In seconds we'll find our claim to fame.

So close your eyes, feel the breeze,
Life's a puzzle, full of tease.
In little moments, find your peace,
In the seconds of laughter, joy will increase.

www.ingramcontent.com/pod-product-compliance
Lightning Source LLC
Chambersburg PA
CBHW051657160426
43209CB00004B/936